MONACO
GRAND PRIX

MONACO GRAND PRIX

Jetty St. John

Lerner Publications Company ▪ Minneapolis

All words printed in **bold** are explained in the glossary.

Front and back cover photographs are by Jeff Bloxham.

Library of Congress Cataloging-in-Publication Data

St. John, Jetty
   Monaco Grand Prix.

   Includes index.
   Summary: Describes the history, rules, course, and recent participants of the Monaco Grand Prix, with an emphasis on the Brazilian driver Nelson Piquet.
   1. Monaco Grand Prix Race — History — Juvenile literature. 2. Piquet, Nelson, 1952-   Juvenile literature. 3. Automobile racing drivers — Brazil — Biography — Juvenile literature. [1. Monaco Grand Prix Race. 2. Automobile racing. 3. Piquet, Nelson, 1952-   ]
GV1034.68.M63M667 1989 796.7'2'0920 [B]   89-2357
ISBN 0-8225-0530-4 (lib. bdg.)

CONTENTS

Martin Brundle, in his Tyrrell, drives the Monaco circuit.

🏁 1 🏁

WELCOME TO MONACO

Each year in May, over 60,000 racing fans flock to **Monaco**, a tiny European country ruled by Prince Rainier III. Some travel in trains that sweep along the Mediterranean coast, past expensive summer homes and sandy beaches. Others climb into helicopters or set sail in private yachts. Still others, in exotic road cars, follow the winding thoroughfares of France toward Monaco.

Racing in the **Grand Prix** is only one of many attractions in Monaco. The little country is famous for its sunny beaches and fashionable residents. At the casino, fortunes have been made and lost in a matter of hours. Luxury yachts cruise the harbor. Early in the morning, the streets become crowded with people following the aroma of fresh-baked bread. At the Hotel de Paris, guests step out of their Ferrari sports cars and disappear into a world of deep carpets, chandeliers, and exquisite flower arrangements.

High on a hill, Prince Rainier's castle overlooks the Mediterranean harbor. From there, the bustling streets below seem narrow and cramped. During race weekend, the streets are sealed off from normal traffic, and the Grand Prix de Monaco takes place. Near the **circuit**, Prince Rainier and his children watch the race from the royal box, and from there the prizes are awarded. Winning is a great honor, but most drivers consider it an achievement just to qualify for the race.

If it were not for all the steep hills

The new chicane at the harbor

and the many cafes that serve delicious, glazed strawberry tarts, one could probably walk around Monaco in a couple of hours. Nelson Piquet (pronounced pee-KAY), a **World Champion** driver, walked from his two-bedroom apartment in Monte Carlo, down to the harbor to examine the new **chicane**. This sharp bend had just been expanded, so it now swung out farther over the water. The old chicane had also been meant to slow down the race cars, but they had still shot around it at 140 miles per hour (225 km/h). Piquet remembered that at this speed he could scarcely see the corners. Now he would have to take this new section in first gear at about 30 miles per hour (48 km/h). He hoped there would be room for passing other cars. Then he looked down and saw that the **camber**, an arch in the cross section of the road, would make passing extremely difficult.

Soon he would be racing 78 laps

An aerial view of Monaco as seen from the castle

around the circuit at speeds over 100 miles per hour (160 km/h). This circuit, slightly more than 161 miles (259 km) long, was shorter than other World Championship courses, so he could drive as fast as he wanted without running out of gas.

Piquet left the chicane and followed the road along the harbor. Then he turned sharply toward the start/finish line. He stopped there and began to picture the beginning of the race. To win he would have to get a good start.

Piquet has driven on circuits all over the world, and he dislikes the Monaco circuit, his home course. "There is a mental bogey attached to it," he has said. Not only are the turns sharp, but the streets are so narrow there is scarcely room for two modern race cars to drive side by side. Overtaking (passing) is extremely difficult—even treacherous—and the short straights make it hard to catch the vehicle in front of you. Piquet

9

Nelson Piquet, **above,** *lives in an apartment in Monaco.*

remembered the collision he had had the year before. Just when he was about to finish his 16th lap, he'd hit the right-hand guard rail near the start/finish line and slammed into the car next to him. Within seconds both vehicles had flipped into the air and landed in the **run-off area** on the side road.

2

MONACO'S HEROES

The Grand Prix (French for grand prize) de Monaco is a tradition that started in 1929 and was broken only during World War II. Jackie Stewart won three races at Monaco, but Graham Hill, who won five, holds the record. Leading the race in 1965, Hill reached the old chicane only to find that the road was blocked by a broken-down car. He was traveling at 95 miles per hour (152 km/h) when he jammed on his brakes and shot down the run-off area. Furiously, he got out of the car to push it back onto the circuit. By then four cars had overtaken him, but with record-breaking speed he passed them and went on to win the race. Now, after five victories, Graham Hill is called the "uncrowned monarch of Monaco."

Nelson Piquet drives for the Williams team. One of his great rivals is Alain Prost, a French driver who races for the McLaren team. Every season Prost and Piquet battle for World Championship points. Close competition between drivers makes racing exciting to watch. Piquet said, "There is nothing better than beating someone you really respect." Prost is a fast, cool-headed driver who hardly ever makes a mistake. Both drivers like to win. Piquet explained, "Once you have tasted success, you want more of it."

Each year, about 16 races take place in the **Formula One** World Championship series. They are held in Europe, Canada, North and South America, and

Ayrton Senna, Lotus Team, above left; *Alain Prost, McLaren Team,* above right; *Stefan Johansson, Ferrari Team,* below left; *and Martin Brundle, Tyrrell Team,* below right

Australia. A dozen or more racing teams travel thousands of miles around the globe to compete. Each race lasts up to two hours. The circuits can be anywhere from 157 to almost 200 miles long (252-322 km).

To score points for the championship, a driver must place among the top six contenders. Points accumulate throughout the year, and at the end of the series, the driver with the most points wins the Formula One World Championship. Prior to the Monaco Grand Prix, three races had taken place. When Piquet won the first race of the season in Brazil, he gained 9 points. The other two races were held in Spain and Italy. In Italy Piquet came in second with 6 points, which gave him a total of 15. Ayrton Senna finished first in Spain and second in Brazil, so he was tied with Piquet for first place in the race to be World Champion. Alain Prost came in third in Spain and first in Italy, so he earned a total of 13 championship points.

Two cars per team also use the same scoring system to gain points toward the Constructor's Cup, the award given to the team whose cars score the most points in the World Championships. The cars win points at each race for being among the first six to cross the finish line.

World Championship Points

Race Position	Points
1st	9
2nd	6
3rd	4
4th	3
5th	2
6th	1

The excitement of racing outweighs any feeling of danger. Piquet noted, however, that a little fear is good. "It prevents me from taking risks that could kill me. It also gets the adrenaline flowing." There are only about six drivers in the world who can consistently win Formula One races. It takes a person with outstanding speed, endurance, and skill to survive such a rigorous sport.

At the first race, in Rio de Janeiro, Brazil, Piquet delighted the crowd when he won. Piquet, who was born in Brazil, enjoys racing in Rio because he always gets a tremendous amount of support from the spectators. Although he was tied for first place, Piquet was not sure

Clean turns around corners can cut seconds off lap times.

how long his luck would last. He knew that Monaco would be a tough race. Prost did extremely well on street circuits, and for the last two years the Frenchman had won the race.

To train for Monaco's Grand Prix, Piquet had test-driven his car for thousands of miles. He had been working with the team designer Patrick Head and the mechanics. They needed to get the angle of the **wings,** the **suspension,** and the gears set right for Monaco. Piquet had practiced hundreds of gear changes, and he had spent hours accelerating and braking at speeds reaching 200 miles an hour (320 km/h). In his mind he kept a picture of Monte Carlo's twisting streets, and he worked hard to increase his speed around the corners. He knew that Prost cut seconds off his lap times by carving clean turns.

3

PORTRAIT OF PIQUET

Piquet's real name is Nelson Souto Maior. He was born in 1952. When he began his racing career, he started using his mother's maiden name, Piquet. He did this to hide the fact that he was racing because his parents wanted him to be a tennis player, not a Grand Prix driver. Piquet started out racing Formula Vee cars, a class of cars built only from parts made by Volkswagen. But by the time he was 25, he was already racing **Formula Three** cars and test-driving the more powerful Formula One cars. In 1979, because of his speed on the track, Nelson was asked to be a Formula One driver, and he has been successful ever since.

Although Nelson Piquet is Brazilian, he lives in Monaco. Not only does the country have a beautiful Mediterranean climate, but the taxes are extremely low. Many drivers choose to live in Europe because road racing has been a tradition there for over 100 years.

Piquet used to drive for a British team called Brabham. During the racing season drivers cannot change teams, but at the end of the year they often switch to a different team for more money or a better car. In 1986, Piquet joined the Williams Formula One team, also based in England. He was sad to leave his friends, but with the Williams team his salary increased,

Piquet in his Williams Honda

and the Honda engine made his car extremely fast. When it is necessary for him to be in England, Piquet can commute from Monaco to London by plane in only two hours.

Piquet is a quiet man with a keen sense of humor. Once, before a race, he secretly put a sticker on Prost's racing suit. The sticker said, "Nelson Piquet Fan Club." When Piquet is not racing, he loves to spend time at his home or on his boat in Monaco. He has a motor cruiser that can go up to 30 mph (48 km/h), and he often invites friends on board. Prost even stayed on the boat once, before going to Italy to visit the Ferrari team.

Unlike Prost and most other drivers, Piquet does not like publicity. Although he is friendly, he puts all his energy into racing. He says he makes enough money driving cars (around $3.3 million a year). He would rather stay in bed than get up early to make more money by doing an advertisement.

Frank Williams, the owner of the team, described Piquet as, "the best driver in the world." Williams was looking for someone who had speed, courage, and an ability to think. Piquet won the World Championship title in 1981, 1983, and more recently, for the Williams team, in 1987. When driving, Piquet has a knack for detecting mechanical problems with his car. This makes him popular with the team's designer and with his mechanics. Piquet also tries to place consistently among the top six cars. He said, "Sometimes I would rather take second place and get some points, than try for an all-out first and get nothing at all."

Other drivers refer to Piquet as "the easygoing Brazilian," but his cheerful manner conceals a highly competitive nature. Once he gets into his car, Piquet wants to go faster than every other driver, including his teammate, Nigel Mansell.

4

GETTING READY

In Monaco, preparations for the Grand Prix began right after Easter. Roads in the course were resurfaced. Workmen took extra care in repairing trouble spots, such as the hill down by the harbor and the flying exit from Casino Square, where the road suddenly slopes down. Cranes were parked at strategic spots around the circuit, in case wrecked cars needed to be removed quickly. New steel guardrails glittered along tight curves and along the narrow straightaways. Work crews constructed grandstands and installed wire netting to catch any parts that might fly from the track into the spectators' area in the event of a crash. All this construction created quite a challenge for Monaco residents, who often had to climb over new railings or detour around race sites to carry on their business.

On Wednesday evening, huge transporters, loaded with race cars, began to roll into the tiny **principality** of Monaco.

Inching their way through the narrow streets to the harbor, they parked at the foothills of the castle. The road was then fenced off to form the **paddock**, an area where the mechanics could work on the cars and the drivers could stay in special road trailers.

A cheer rang out as the red nose of a Ferrari crept from under the canvas awning of its truck. Thousands of fans, especially those from Italy, wanted a look. The Ferrari Formula One is known, because of its emblem, as the *Prancing Horse*.

Williams mechanics work on Nigel Mansell's Honda, **above,** *and a Ferrari designer talks with mechanics,* **below.**

A Williams mechanic with engine and chassis, left; *Martin Brundle in his Tyrrell,* below.

Piquet searched for the yellow and blue of his own transporter. By the time he found it, his car had been removed from the truck. He admired the car's streamlined shape, specially designed to cut swiftly through the air. The whole vehicle was light and strong, and the tires were wide so they could grip the road. The suspension had also been adjusted so that when Piquet braked, cornered, or accelerated, the car would be set for Monaco's twisting circuit.

Piquet talked with the mechanics about his engine. Some teams use two engines. One is a thirsty qualifying engine that is built for speed during a few fast laps. The other, a more reliable, fuel-efficient race engine, is slower and is built to cover distance. Piquet's team has qualifying engines but decided not to use them. Each team only had time to set up one type of engine, and Piquet's team decided to get the engine and car ready for the actual race.

Soon Piquet saw the the dark, curly hair and small, muscular body of his friend Alain Prost. The Frenchman was heading toward his red and white McLaren, known for its fine, **aerodynamic** shape and its **TAG**/Porsche engine. Piquet knew that his own car, with a Honda **V6 Turbo** engine, was fuel-efficient and powerful on wide, sweeping courses. But he did not know how well it would perform on a circuit that looked a lot like a roller coaster.

When Prost saw Piquet, he called out, "The Williams car will do well at Monaco, but if it doesn't, then the Championship will be closer." This year Prost was determined to beat Jackie Stewart's record of winning 26 Grands Prix. Prost had already won twice at Monaco, so he felt confident about racing on the street circuit. His car was fast and reliable. If he could get a good place on the **starting grid**, the race would be his.

Prost has been described by racing specialists as "a complete driver." He does extremely well on both open courses and street circuits. Even in bad weather conditions, he rarely makes a mistake. Racing is his life, and, like Piquet, he cannot imagine choosing another career. To relax, Prost plays golf. He also thoroughly enjoys skiing in Switzerland, where he has his home.

5

THE PRACTICE RACE

On Thursday morning the mechanics prepared the cars for an untimed practice race. During this 90-minute session, the drivers test their cars and get a feel for the course.

The cars were taken over to the **pits**, which form a road on the side of the track. Here, each team can fit new tires or do minor repairs to its vehicles during a race. The cars hurtle in and out of the pits at high speeds, and even the mechanics find it a dangerous place because it is easy to be hit.

Piquet drove his car out onto the track and raced around the twisting circuit. With each lap, he tried to increase his speed, but after a while he returned to the pits. The car was too slow coming out of the turns.

His vehicle had been rigged with sophisticated electronic equipment that sent information to computers set up in the pits. Team designer Patrick Head was studying the computer printout, to see if the wrong tires had been used, if the suspension needed adjusting, or if the **airfoils** (or wings) should be set at a different angle. Piquet felt there might also be a problem with the gears.

The angle of the wings, or airfoils, is especially important on a twisting circuit like Monaco. The wings on a car act like upside-down airplane wings. Instead of lifting the vehicle in the air, they force it down toward the track. Wings must be angled so that air rushing by the car creates a downforce. This downforce

increases the grip of the tires, which makes the car more stable and enables it to accelerate more quickly. This force pushes the tires onto the road and helps the car to corner. If the angle of the wings is too great, the air pressure will hold the car back. When a balance is reached, the car can grip the corners and still give a good chase on the flat, where the road is straight.

On paper, a car may seem perfectly designed for the circuit, but when the driver tests it, the car may not respond the way the driver would like. And all drivers have their own techniques. After the practice session, for example, Prost asked his mechanics to angle the wings up more. With his McLaren "glued" to the road, Prost can drive a neat line around the corners without skidding sideways. However, his teammate, Keke Rosberg, wanted the mechanics to lessen some of the wing angle. Rosberg's car might slide around the corners, but it would rocket down the straight parts of the road.

Like Prost, Piquet preferred plenty of downforce on the back wing. Not only would it help him with cornering, but also with braking, especially in places like the new chicane.

The wing angles on Piquet's Williams Honda, **left,** *compared to those on a Ferrari,* **right**

6

QUALIFYING—A MATTER OF TIRES AND TIMING

Because split-second accuracy is so important in Grands Prix races, speeds must be measured exactly. The lap speeds of each car are monitored by the Longine timing system. Over 70 years ago this Swiss company timed skiing, swimming, and running at the Olympics. In 1933, it timed the first Grand Prix in Brazil, and in 1981, it became the permanent timekeeper for Formula One racing.

As soon as each car arrives on the circuit, a black electronic "coder" box, the size of a bar of soap, is attached to it. The coder box gives out a different signal for each car. The signal is picked up by a receiver at the start/finish line. Accurate to 1/1000 of a second, the receiver flashes lap speeds onto a computer screen. On race day it also shows a frame-by-frame picture of the finish. A picture is useful when two cars come in close together.

For qualifying sessions, the cars are allowed to use only two sets of soft tires, which are marked by race officials. The smooth, sticky rubber of the special tires grips the road, and the cars go even faster than they do on race day. The drivers, however, can only do a few laps before these special tires wear out.

For a course like Monaco, Goodyear supplies each of its teams, including Piquet's, with at least 20 sets of Eagle racing tires. These sets range from super-sticky qualifying tires, which look bald, to deeply grooved tires, for use in the rain. All the tires are specially designed

Tires are the topic of discussion, above and below right.

to handle the heavy braking, turning, and accelerating that happen on a street circuit.

Choosing the right tires can mean the difference between winning and losing a Grand Prix. The weather, the air temperature, the surface of the track, and the way the tires heat up during practice are all carefully monitored in the pits. Based on this information, which is transmitted to a computer, the team's owner, the designer, and the drivers work together to decide whether to use hard, medium, or soft rubber tires.

7

ONE LAP IS ALL IT TAKES TO QUALIFY

There are two qualifying sessions for the Monaco Grand Prix, one on Thursday afternoon and one on Saturday. To earn a place on the starting grid, drivers (or "pilots" as they are called in Europe) race against the clock. The person who drives the fastest single lap wins the **pole position**, which is the best starting place—on the inside front row of the starting line. From that position, not only does the car travel a shorter distance around the corners, but once the car is in the lead, the sharp turns and narrow straightaways make it hard for the other cars to catch up.

One of the problems with the qualifying sessions at Monaco is that the narrow course becomes littered with disabled cars. Because of the difficult nature of the track, there is a lot more wear and tear on a car's transmission (gear box) and brakes. A vehicle at Monaco, therefore, is more likely to break down than it is on other more open courses. Out on the course, drivers may find that they have to weave around other vehicles that have broken down. If cars are blocking the road, there are delays while crews mop up spilled oil, and cranes lift damaged vehicles from the track. Once the all clear is given, the remaining cars scramble to complete their laps.

During the qualifying session on Saturday afternoon, Piquet's car was one of the vehicles that broke down. After a few laps, his engine blew up and sprayed the road with oil. Returning to the pits,

A crane removes a disabled Tyrrell from the track, above. Alain Prost in his McLaren, below

Nigel Mansel, Piquet's teammate, in his Williams Honda, right; *Williams mechanics working in the paddock,* below

A Williams mechanic adjusts Piquet's car.

he switched to the spare car, but it soon developed gear problems. The Williams cars were not standing up at all well to Monaco's tight corners, especially those along the new chicane. Patrick Head sighed, but he assured Piquet that the team mechanics would have his car repaired before the race, which was two weeks away. To run properly, the engine needed some special parts, which Head said he would get. In spite of problems, Piquet still managed to complete one qualifying lap.

Twenty cars would compete in the Grand Prix, and Alain Prost's car would be one of them. Prost had known that if he captured the pole position by setting the fastest qualifying time, he would probably win the race. He had been on his second set of qualifying tires when he reached his fifth lap. When he accelerated, he was amazed to find the road so clear. In just over one minute and 22 seconds, Prost, the McLaren driver, had managed to do the fastest lap of all the contenders. The pole position was his. Piquet, although disappointed with the performance of his car, still managed to get 11th place on the starting grid.

After the qualifying session, the mechanics of each team rolled the cars back to the paddock. There, they removed the fast qualifying engines and replaced them with the more reliable, less thirsty engines that are built to race for two hours. Because Piquet had used the race engine during the qualifying race, the mechanics did not have to replace the engine, but they still broke it down to clean it, tune it, and replace some of its parts.

8

WHO PAYS THE BILLS?

One million dollars of prize money is put up by the organizers of each race. The Automobile Club de Monaco pays for the principality's Grand Prix. After the race, the prize money is split among the winning drivers. When Piquet won the race in Brazil, for example, he got $50,000 plus extra money for leading many of the laps during the race. The drivers give the money to their teams because they already get large salaries. Prizes, however, provide only about 10 percent of the money needed by Formula One teams. Most of the money comes from sponsors.

Monaco attracts many sponsors from all over the world. Sponsors are representatives from large companies that provide teams with money or parts in return for advertising or technical information. While the cars were racing around the course, many sponsors got together to arrange business contracts with the various teams. Without spon-

sors, Formula One teams would find it difficult to survive. A successful team like Williams costs at least $20 million a year to run, even though Goodyear supplies the team with free tires, and, in 1986, Honda provided the engines. That's why Piquet's car is often called the Williams/Honda. If drivers like Piquet and Prost are among the top six Grand Prix drivers, each of their salaries will start at $3 million a year.

Piquet's white racing suit is covered with badges showing the names and

A Ferrari, with its transporter to the rear

symbols of the companies that sponsor his team. They include ICI, Mobil, Goodyear, Canon, and Denim. Each badge costs a company about $70,000. Ten years ago Piquet wore a wreath around his neck after he won a race. Now the wreath is omitted because sponsors want their logos to show—especially in front of the television cameras.

Even Ferrari, one of the richest teams, has sponsors. The Marlboro company pays Ferrari an amount equal to the salaries of the team's two top drivers just to paste a small Marlboro sticker on the side of the famous car. Agip, an Italian petroleum company, supplies the team's fuel, and Goodyear provides the tires. Fiat also has its name on the side of the car.

Frequently, drivers and their cars also display the colors of their main sponsor. Prost, for example, wears a red driving suit for Marlboro, and his car is red and white. To match his car, Lotus driver Ayrton Senna wears a black and gold suit, the colors of John Player Special, the tobacco company that sponsors his team.

Sponsors know that Formula One racing receives the third largest sports coverage in the world. (The Olympics is first and World Cup Soccer second.) More than 20 countries watch the races each year, and the audience is about 935 million. Sponsors like drivers such as Piquet because he speaks fluent English, and his car is usually up at the front of a race where the television cameras are focused.

Ayrton Senna in his Lotus

Piercarlo Ghinzani in his Osella

9

ACCIDENTS AND DANGERS

Formula One racing, because it is such a dangerous and competitive sport, is controlled by many rules and regulations. Race specialists from all over the world work together to decide the proper shape, size, weight, and horsepower for Formula One cars. Each team has its own design, but rivals watch each other closely to see that the cars conform to the rules. The amount of fuel each car may carry is also an important decision. With less fuel, speeds drop to safer levels because drivers must conserve gas to complete the course. Formula One rules are always being updated, especially if a change will make the races less dangerous.

Accidents in Grand Prix racing can be violent, and sometimes fatal. For example, in 1955, Alberto Ascari was racing his Lancia toward the Monaco harbor when he lost control. In those days, there were no steel barriers to stop him, and Ascari spun over the low wall

and crashed into the water. Both car and driver disappeared into the sea, but Ascari soon came to the surface. Apart from a few bruises and a broken nose, he was all right. But to this day boats must move away from that spot during races, and a team of scuba divers stands ready in case an accident occurs.

In 1962, Colin Chapman, the late owner of the Lotus team, asked his designers to build a **monocoque**, or super-strong cockpit, to protect the driver. He encouraged other Formula One designers

The steering wheel can be removed in five seconds so the driver can get out quickly.

Fire marshals helped when Andrea de Cesaris' Minardi spilled oil on the track.

to do the same. The driver sits in the monocoque, which is made of special materials reinforced with **carbon fiber**. The material can be molded, and it is strong, light, and easy to repair. The monocoque, with the engine and fuel tank, forms an integral part of the **chassis**. In Piquet's car the engine is crammed into a small space. Some parts are only a few millimeters away from the bodywork. Behind him there are 195 liters (51 gallons) of high octane gasoline. During the race, Formula One cars get about 3.8 miles (6.11 kilometers) to the gallon. The gasoline is in a special fuel cell which won't burst during a crash.

In 1960, before the days of seat belts, Cliff Allison was racing his Ferrari at Monaco when he hit the curb on the side of the chicane. Allison was thrown out of the car, and he woke up to find himself in the hospital. He remembered that, by accident, he had changed from fifth to second gear. The back wheels had locked and the car had spun out. Later in the '60s, however, Jackie Stewart began wearing seat belts, and he worked hard to promote their use in both racing cars and ordinary road cars. Today, Formula One drivers are secured by two shoulder straps, two thigh straps, and one stomach strap. Soon head restraints may also be used.

Since the time of Hill and Stewart, steel barriers have replaced the bales of straw on the sides of the road. Apart from that, the course has not changed much over the years, but the cars have. Niki Lauda, another well-known driver who won the race in 1975, said, "Here I am rushing round exactly the same circuit that I drove 11 years ago, and yet my car is twice as powerful." Monaco's twisting circuit has always provided an element of danger. Although the old cars were much slower, they were not as safe as the faster, modern race cars.

In the old, cigar-shaped race cars, drivers used to sit with their shoulders above the car. Today, if a car flips, two roll bars keep the driver's head and hands off the road. The roll bars can hold seven and a half times the weight of the driver and the car with a full tank of gas.

Fire poses another danger. Drivers sit in their cars with over 51 gallons (195 liters) of fuel tucked behind them. To help the driver get out in a hurry, safety harnesses have quick-release mechanisms, and steering wheels can be easily removed. A kill switch in the cockpit shuts off all electrical circuits. The

Before the days of seat belts, Cliff Allison was thrown from his Ferrari when it hit the side of the chicane.

Jonathan Palmer pulls on his balaclava.

smallest flame triggers two automatic fire extinguishers, which give the engine and the cockpit a good soaking. A small tube also connects the driver's helmet to an emergency supply of oxygen which may save a life.

As a precaution against fire, Piquet, like other drivers, wears regulation clothing made of flame-proof materials. Next to his skin, he wears special socks, long johns, a sweater, and a balaclava (a knit cap for the head and neck). His racing suit is made up of many layers, which offer greater protection from flames and high temperatures. The suit is made so it will not rip, melt, or give off poisonous gases. On his feet, he wears lightweight racing boots. Last of all, he puts on his gloves and a helmet.

As another precaution, fire marshals are posted every few yards along the circuit. They also dress in fire-resistant clothing, and they carry fire extinguishers. A fire truck and a wrecking crew are normally on the scene of an accident within 30 seconds after it happens. Sometimes if a car flips upside down, it has to be turned over, and pieces may have to be cut away from it before the driver can be rescued. Doctors and a neurosurgeon are rushed to the scene of an accident, and helicopters fly injured persons to the hospital.

The chances of a driver having an accident are about one in ten Grands Prix. During his practice session in Brazil, Piquet was getting ready to take a corner at high speed when one of his back tires went off the road, and he skidded on the grass. He spun across the track and hit the curb. His car turned over in the air and almost landed upside down on the track. But Piquet was lucky; he only bruised his wrist.

The fire retardant suit of a Benetton driver, left; *Stefan Johansson wearing his fire retardant underwear,* right.

Piquet racing in his Williams Honda

🏁 10 🏁

ABOUT TO BEGIN

Although he knew how tough the competition would be, Piquet still tried to relax in the Williams road trailer. It was Sunday, two hours before the race. Mechanics were making last-minute adjustments to his car. Just outside, Piquet could hear the voices of his sponsors as they sat under the trailer awning, enjoying a fine lunch of cheeses, fruit, paté, chicken, and champagne. In the grandstands, spectators were buying large, French bread sandwiches as they jostled their way toward good seats. After a while, however, everything grew quiet. It seemed as if the whole town was waiting for the race to begin.

When Piquet left the trailer, he was determined to pick up at least one championship point. Before he even got into his car, Piquet's pulse began to increase from a normal 70 beats per minute to 100 beats per minute. He remembered the qualifying race and thought that Monaco's course was tricky

enough without having to deal with engine troubles.

Piquet pulled on his balaclava, followed by his helmet. Last of all, he put on his gloves, which almost reached to his elbows. Except for his eyes peering through his visor, not an inch of flesh was visible. Half an hour before the race, he climbed into his car. There was hardly room to move in the cockpit, so his mechanics helped fasten the safety harnesses. Because the day was clear and sunny, Piquet could see a long way

As the crowd watches, Piquet steers his car around a corner near the harbor.

down the road. He did not notice the mass of spectators. His attention was focused on the first corner.

Once on the circuit, Piquet steered his car toward the others as they glided slowly around the course. He swerved from side to side, not to alarm the other drivers, but to warm up his tires so they would grip better. In the pits, fresh tires were kept warm for him in special electric blankets, so when he came in for a quick tire change, they would be ready for use.

As he autographs a program, right, Stefan Johansson says, "Nice hat." The young fan's hat says "Ferrari," Johansson's team. Below, racing fans shop for souvenirs.

Piquet, **above**, *knows that racing takes tremendous stamina and concentration.*

As Piquet approached the starting line, his pulse jumped to 175 beats a minute. During the race it would peak at 200. An ordinary man or woman would have to run a 100-yard dash to reach the same pulse rate. Racing a car for two hours requires tremendous stamina and concentration. There are hundreds of gear changes to make. While cornering, the car follows the curve in the road, but Piquet's body still travels in a straight line. It feels as if the foot pedals are ripping sideways, away from him, and he has to fight to keep his feet in place. Under the bright sun of Monaco the cockpit grows hotter and hotter. Racing is thirsty work. Piquet said, "When I first started in Formula One, I used to feel physically and mentally exhausted after only 15 laps." Once he even fainted on the winner's rostrum.

Piquet, above, *placed second at San Marino, in April.*

Formula One cars accelerate from 0 to 100 mph (160 km/h) in 10 seconds. Above, Piquet is followed by Johansson.

🏁 11 🏁
THE RACE

After the preliminary warm-up rounds, the cars were ushered onto the starting grid, two by two. An official for each pair of cars signaled that all was well. Alain Prost took pole position, which gave him a huge advantage at Monaco. Once he pulled away from the rest of the pack, the narrow turns would make him difficult to catch. Prost knew that the drivers behind him would struggle to pass one another, and in so doing they would soon wear out their cars' engines and brakes. Alongside Prost was Piquet's teammate, Nigel Mansell. Ayrton Senna, in his Lotus, was starting third.

Seconds after the cars got into position, the starting light changed from red to green. Thundering noise from the engines shook nearby buildings. Suddenly the air smelled like a mixture of rubber and burning toast. In one dizzying moment, all 20 racing machines flashed by.

From the 11th position on the starting grid, Piquet battled to escape the thick crowd of cars at the beginning of the race. Chances of crashing before the first corner, at Sainte Devote, were extremely high. Having cleared that stretch, he accelerated up the hill toward the Hotel de Paris. To Piquet, who was traveling at 170 miles per hour (272 km/h) when entering Casino Square, the palm trees outside the hotel seemed to be just a blur. He flew onto the downhill stretch toward the Hotel Mirabeau.

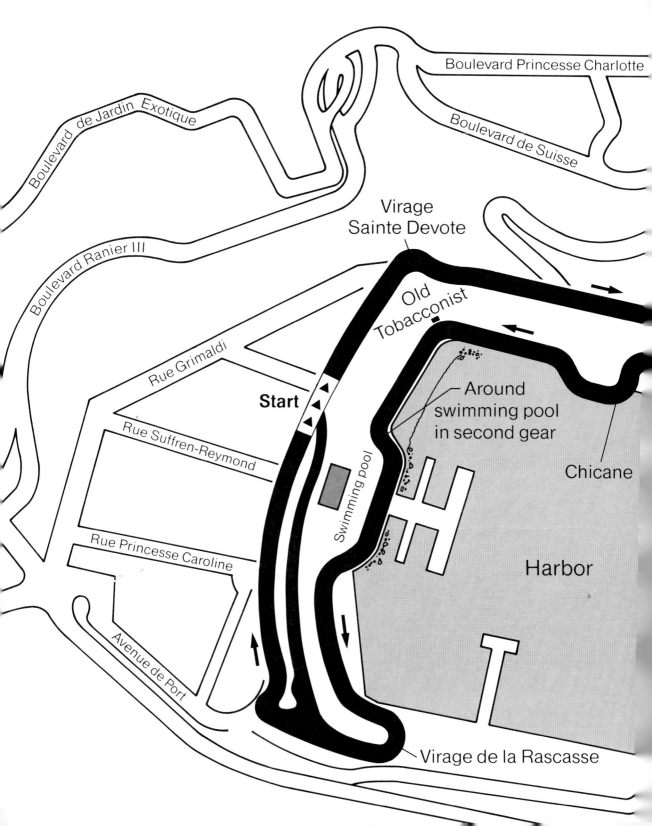

Boulevard Princesse Charlotte

Boulevard de Jardin Exotique

Boulevard de Suisse

Boulevard Ranier III

Virage Sainte Devote

Old Tobacconist

Rue Grimaldi

Start

Around swimming pool in second gear

Rue Suffren-Reymond

Swimming pool

Chicane

Rue Princesse Caroline

Harbor

Avenue de Port

Virage de la Rascasse

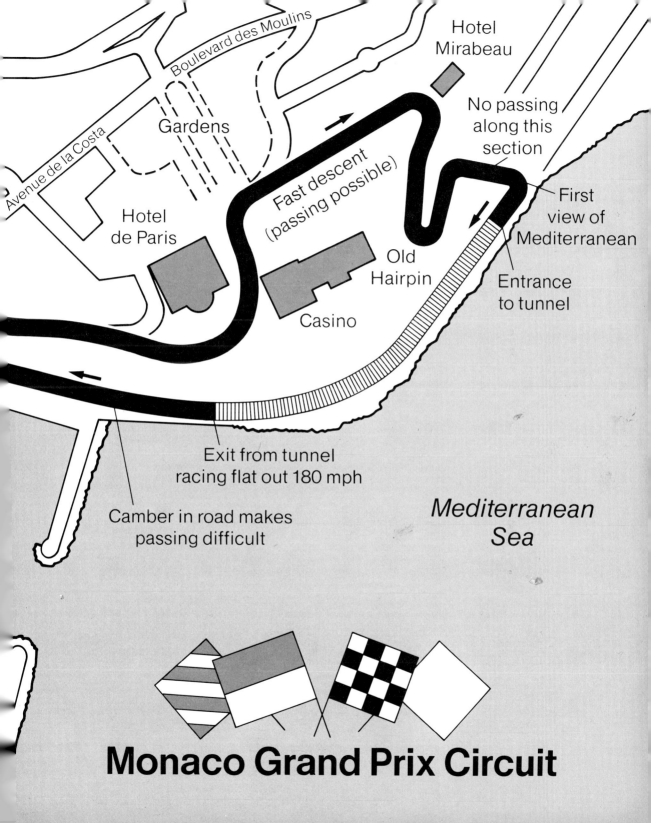

Monaco Grand Prix Circuit

A Ferrari winds around a hairpin curve near the Loews Hotel.

This was one of the few places where passing was possible. All the drivers accelerated hard.

Piquet braked, then changed quickly into second gear for a series of tight bends. The hairpin turn by the Loews Hotel came first. Passing was impossible in this section. Suddenly, he saw a bright blue patch of the Mediterranean Sea. Moments later, as he plunged into the shadows of a tunnel, he accelerated to 180 miles per hour (288 km/h).

After the tunnel, the way seemed clear, but because of the camber, no one passed. Piquet knew that he would have to slow down rapidly for the chicane.

Using a low gear, he crept around this section. Once free of the curve, he headed toward another famous landmark, the Old Tobacconist.

To complete one full circuit, Piquet still had to pass the public swimming pool. He then took a tight corner at the Virage de la Rascasse before going up a short section, in first gear, to the start/finish line.

Piquet had moved up from 11th place on the grid. Now he was fighting to move from behind Martin Brundle, who was in seventh place. Battles among Brundle, Piquet, and another driver, Patrick Tambay, continued throughout the race.

Nigel Mansell, Piquet's teammate, passes the casino, above. *On the* left, *Martin Brundle (Tyrrell) is pursued by Patrick Tambay (Haas).*

Tambay's Haas mounted Brundle's car, and one wheel of the Haas grazed Brundle's helmet.

The battles were briefly interrupted by a tire change on the 33rd lap. For spectators, this chase was the most exciting part of the race. Finally, on the 68th lap, Piquet slipped past Brundle.

Tambay tried to do the same on the section near the Mirabeau. The two cars—a Haas and a Tyrrell—moved closer and closer together. On the inside lane, Tambay, the French driver of the red Haas, tried to squeeze by the white Tyrrell, driven by Brundle, an Englishman. The white Tyrrell continued on its course until the front left corner of the

The Haas somersaulted in midair and hit a guard rail before landing back on the track.

red Haas mounted it. Brundle's helmet was grazed by a tire before his opponent's car did a somersault in mid-air. The car dented the guard rail and landed back on the road.

A yellow flag was waved, and several marshals ran out to help the stunned drivers. A rather bruised Patrick Tambay climbed out of the cockpit and hurried to safety behind the barrier. Martin Brundle drove slowly back to the pits with his engine damaged. He thought he was lucky to be alive.

Piquet gained seventh place, but gear problems made it difficult to accelerate out of corners.

Ayrton Senna checks lap speeds on a computer screen.

Keke Rosberg, Prost's teammate, finished second in Monaco.

Meanwhile, Piquet had gained a place, and he continued his pursuit of the driver in front of him. His strength was being taxed. Although his car was slow on the corners, it suddenly jolted him as it picked up speed on the straights.

When the yellow flag was waved,

temporarily limiting the race, Prost slowed down, but he was still in the lead. By starting first, Prost had had a clear road ahead of him, and he had saved wear on his gear box and brakes. Prost temporarily lost the lead to Ayrton Senna when, on the 35th lap, he went into the pits for fresh tires. Soon, however, Prost regained first place and won his third Monaco Grand Prix in a row. The only other man to have done this was Graham Hill, who won in 1963, 1964, and 1965. In his smooth-running car, Prost had driven a perfect race. Out of the hundreds of gear shifts, he had not missed one, and his tire change during the pit stop had been incredibly quick. The McLaren team had done extremely well.

Prost's teammate, Keke Rosberg, finished second, and Ayrton Senna, in his Lotus, was third. The three drivers went to the Royal Box to be congratulated by Prince Rainier and two of his children, Prince Albert and Princess Stephanie. In the tradition of Formula One, corks were popped, and champagne sprayed into the air.

Just missing a championship point, Piquet was happy to finish in seventh place. Gear troubles had made it hard for him to accelerate out of the corners, and his tires were nearly ruined. He knew, however, that once his car was running properly again, he would win more races. Before the Monaco Grand Prix, Piquet and Senna had been tied for first place in World Championship points. Prost had now taken the lead, Senna was second,

and Piquet was third.

The Monaco Grand Prix was over for another year. By evening, the cars were back in their transporters. The smell of suntan lotion had disappeared from the grandstands. The streets were hosed down with fresh water, and showers of fireworks splashed into the Mediterranean. As the last train pulled out, filled with spectators, Piquet walked back to his home.

Postscript

The final race of the 1986 Formula One World Championship was in Adelaide, South Australia. Alain Prost became World Champion for the second time. Nelson Piquet was third behind his teammate Nigel Mansell. The following year, however, Piquet took the title, which made him a three-time World Champion. The Brazilian now drives for the Lotus team, which is also based in England.

The three winners, from left to right, Senna, Prost, and Rosberg, celebrate in the Royal Box. Prince Rainier is standing behind Rosberg.

After the Monaco Grand Prix, the spectators leave and the streets return to normal as the last train departs.

APPENDIX

Teams

(In 1986, because of the narrow course, only 20 of these cars were allowed to race at Monaco. Since then, the rules have been changed, allowing a greater number to compete.)

McLaren

1	2
Alain Prost	Keke Rosberg

Tyrrell

3	4
Martin Brundle	Philippe Streiff

Williams

5	6
Nigel Mansell	Nelson Piquet

Brabham

7	8
Riccardo Partese	Elio de Angelis

Lotus

11	12
John Dumfries	Ayrton Senna

Zakspeed

14
Jonathan Palmer

Haas

15	16
Alan Jones	Patrick Tambay

Arrows

17	18
Marc Surer	Thierry Boutsen

Benetton

19	20
Teo Fabi	Gerhard Berger

Osella

21	22
Piercarlo Ghinzani	Christian Danner

Minardi

23	24
Andrea de Cesaris	Alessandro Nannini

Loto

25	26
René Arnoux	Jacques Laffite

Ferrari

27	28
Michele Alboreto	Stefan Johansson

GLOSSARY

aerodynamic: Streamlined; effectively using the flow of air on and around a moving object. To decrease a Formula One car's resistance to wind and make it aerodynamic, the car is designed to have a streamlined shape.

airfoils: See *wings*.

camber: An arch in the cross section of the road that makes the road high in center and low at the sides

carbon fiber: A high-tech material made from thin strands of carbon. It is strong, light, and easy to repair.

chassis: The major structural component of a car

chicane: A bend in the road designed to slow cars down

circuit: A course, closed to normal traffic, around which the Formula One cars race

Constructor's Cup: An award given to a team whose cars score the highest number of points in the World Championships

Formula One: A set of rules in World Championship Grand Prix racing. The rules control the design of the car, the engine, the safety features, the weight, the fuel capacity, and also the type of circuit used. Formula One cars are the ultimate in single-seat race cars.

Formula Three: A set of rules which puts more limitations on car design than Formula One rules. Formula Three cars are smaller and have less power than Formula One cars.

Grand Prix: The term developed from the name of the first Grande Epreuve or grand test races in France. The term *Grand Prix* eventually grew to mean *Grand Prize*. This usually refers to Formula One events, but the term is also used in other types of racing.

Monaco: One of the smallest countries in the world (0.73 square miles or 1.9 square kilometers). It is bordered by the Mediterranean Sea on one side and by France on the other three sides.

monocoque: A survival cell designed to protect the driver. It also forms part of the front chassis.

paddock: An enclosed area where the transporters are parked, teams can keep spare parts, and mechanics can repair cars

pits: A side road on the edge of the circuit where, during the race, each team can fit new tires, or do minor repairs to its cars

pole position: The best position, at the inner front of the starting grid

principality: Country or territory ruled by a prince

run-off area: A stretch of ground or a side road where a car can get off the racing circuit and out of the way of other cars

starting grid: Area of the circuit from which the cars begin the race

suspension: A system to stabilize the car as it changes speed or direction. It also counteracts the effect of irregularities in the road surface.

TAG: *TAG* stands for Technic Avant-Garde, which is the name of a company that has worked with Porsche to develop the McLaren engine.

Turbo: Refers to the term *turbocharged,* which is a means of increasing the amount of air flow and pressure to a car's engine for higher performance. For safety reasons, this type of engine is no longer used in Formula One racing.

V6: A term that indicates that the car has six cylinders arranged in a V shape

wings: Mechanisms shaped to create a lift as they travel through air. On a race car, the wings are similar to upside down airplane wings so the wind creates a downforce and pushes the car onto the road. This downforce increases the grip of the tires on the road and gives the car more stability. Wings are also called airfoils.

World Champion: A title won each year by a Formula One driver, who scores the most points out of approximately 16 races

Index

ABOUT THE AUTHOR

Jetty St. John has been writing for young people for over 10 years and has had several books published. While working at the University of Minnesota, she developed materials on topics ranging from bicycle safety to teen car crashes. Her interest in motor racing began over 20 years ago, while she was living in England. St. John has traveled through South America and Europe as a writer, and she now lives in the Twin Cities with her son and daughter.

ACKNOWLEDGMENTS: The photographs in this book are by Jeff Bloxham, except those on the following pages: p. 37 courtesy of Cliff Allison; pp. 52, 53 Reuters/Bettmann Newsphotos; pp. 14, 25, 26, 27, 42, 59 Jetty St. John.

Front and back cover photographs are by Jeff Bloxham.

The illustration on pages 48-49 is by Laura Westlund.